FINDING
gratitude

A Guided Journal to Help You
Notice the Good in Every Day

WRITTEN BY MIRIAM HATHAWAY · DESIGNED BY SARAH FORSTER

this is the start OF A JOURNEY TO RECOGNIZE WHAT IS ALL AROUND YOU— A LIFE FULL OF GIFTS, BIG AND SMALL.

We tend to search for fulfillment in things outside ourselves—things to get, things to check off our list, things to change. All in pursuit of contentment. Yet you already have what you need to discover happiness.

This journal was created to help you see the good already present in your life. Inside these pages, you'll explore new ways to see everyday gifts, connect with those around you, look forward to simple pleasures, and take comfort in what you already have. As you start to notice these things, your life will change into something richer, stronger, and more rewarding. And the more you practice, the easier it will get—and the healthier and happier you'll become.

So how do you get there? How do you find gratitude? It's already within you, and it's been there all along. IT'S JUST BEEN WAITING FOR YOU TO NOTICE IT.

I feel grateful for...

Gratitude can transform common days into thanksgivings, turn routine jobs into joy, and change ordinary opportunities into blessings.

WILLIAM ARTHUR WARD

invest in your happiness

Gratitude builds us up for life's inevitable ups and downs. As we practice gratitude, we become more optimistic, think more creatively, and have more loving, joyful relationships. Simply put, gratitude means happiness. And happy people have been shown to live longer, healthier lives, and are more resilient to stress and depression. By practicing gratitude, we are investing in a richer, more rewarding life.

SENSE *happiness*

Something wonderful I touched today was...

_____

Someone I enjoyed talking to today was...

_____

A sound I heard today that will stay with me was...

_____

The best thing I smelled today was...

_____

The most beautiful thing I saw today was...

_____

see beauty
in FRIENDS

MY CLOSEST FRIEND IS MOST LIKE:

☐ A mountaintop, because she/he is strong, wise, and brings new viewpoints.

☐ A lake, because she/he is deep, contemplative, and peaceful.

☐ A forest, because she/he is full of life, adventurous, and provides refuge.

I feel grateful for...

We often take for granted the very things that most deserve our gratitude. CYNTHIA OZICK

There is a
calmness to a life
lived in gratitude,
a quiet joy.

~ RALPH H. BLUM

notice each moment

It's easy to get weighed down with the mundane and routine things in our lives. But it's a worthwhile challenge to look at them with new eyes. Today, take a moment before each task, breathe in deeply, and acknowledge something about the task that you appreciate. Maybe it's the comforting whir of the coffee grinder. The soap that smells just right. The radio station you listen to every morning. Remember that each new day brings a chance for a new perspective.

What were some of the things you noticed today? How do these things make you feel? What was different about today after noticing them?

take life at your own pace

We often get distracted by looking at others' lives. It seems like someone always has something that we long for, leaving us feeling envious or dissatisfied. We tell ourselves, "If only I had a bigger house. If only I got that promotion. If only I were healthier." Catch yourself each time you say these things, and find a way to remind yourself that you may be exactly where you need to be, and that your path is your own.

I feel grateful for...

times our own light goes out and is rekindled by a spark from
other person. Each of us has cause to think with deep gratitude
those who have lighted the flame within us. ALBERT SCHWEITZER

RECOGNIZE *who's* *cheering for you*

Think of those in your life, those who believe in you, who give you courage, who build you up. Maybe it's a partner, a boss, a close friend. Write down the names of those people who give you strength.

_____

_____

_____

I feel grateful for...

vou concentrate on finding whatever is good in every situation,
u will discover that your life will suddenly be filled with gratitude,
eeling that nurtures the soul. HAROLD KUSHNER

ACT IN *happiness*

Smiles are the universal sign of happiness. A simple smile can improve your mood, even when you don't feel like it. Just by smiling, your brain senses relief from stress and sends messages to your body that you are happy. What are three things that made you smile today?

SMILE #1 _____

SMILE #2 _____

SMILE #3 _____

honor your body

Our bodies are the vessels that carry us and help us experience the world around us. Take a moment to nurture and appreciate your body today. Pick out a favorite pair of earrings or your most comfortable shoes. Before a meal, give thanks to your body for turning the food into energy for the day. Or perhaps as you are falling asleep, wish your body a peaceful rest.

How are you grateful for your body? What did it allow you to do today? How did you give thanks to it?

discover what you care about

Our beliefs and values direct how we live our lives and shape who we are. Think of values that you hold deeply, such as equality, loyalty to friends and family, or service to others. Knowing what you care about most helps you clarify what your priorities are and lead a richer, more fulfilling life. By identifying these, you build cornerstones for your life to guide you in decision making, communicating, and achieving your ambitions.

I feel grateful for...

Gratitude happens when some kindness exceeds expectations, when it is undeserved. Gratitude is a sort of laughter of the heart that comes about after some surprising kindness. DAVID BROOKS

This is a wonderful day. I've never seen this one before.

~MAYA ANGELOU

ACKNOWLEDGE
everyday gifts

There are gifts all around you, though sometimes we take them for granted. Look at the list below and circle all that you are grateful for (and it could be all of them):

1) A comfortable home

2) The freedom to express my opinions

3) Clean clothes and shoes that fit

4) Fresh, running water

5) A friend I can call anytime

6) Time in the day to relax (even for just ten minutes)

7) Access to art (perhaps a statue on a street corner or a painting in an airport)

8) A good book to read

9) _____

10) _____

offer YOUR TALENTS

It may sometimes be hard to remember, but you have many talents. Perhaps it's baking, painting, making others laugh, organizing, or even stargazing. Every talent can turn into a gift—such as giving a neighbor a homemade pie, cheering up a friend, or cleaning up a common space at your work. By offering your talents to others, you'll feel good sharing who you are with the world. SHARE A GIFT WITH SOMEONE TODAY.

What did you share? _____

Who did you share it with? _____

How did they respond when you shared your gift? _____

_____

How did you feel afterwards? _____

_____

I feel grateful for...

ppiness always looks small while you hold it in your hands, but let
o, and you learn at once how big and precious it is. MAXIM GORKY

outweigh THE negative

Think of a significant relationship in your life: a partner, parent, coworker, or close friend. When you know someone well, it's easy to find things to complain about, things that annoy you about them. And it's okay to acknowledge these frustrations. Today, however, make a point to notice the things you appreciate about that person, and give thanks to them for what they bring into your life.

Someone important in my life: _____

What I appreciate about them:

_____

_____

_____

_____

_____

_____

_____

_____

_____

_____

_____

_____

_____

_____

_____

_____

_____

_____

_____

_____

_____

I feel grateful for...

en we focus on our gratitude, the tide of disappointment es out and the tide of love rushes in. KRISTIN ARMSTRONG

find joy in the everyday

We are conditioned to believe that money is the main measure of success. Yet people who have been both rich and poor say that their happiness didn't change with their incomes, just their circumstances. Start to notice the things you already have that bring joy and comfort to your life. Because everyone can be happy. Everyone has it in them. Lasting joy is seeing beauty and finding gratitude in the everyday, no matter how much your paycheck is.

TURN *opportunities* *into* GRATITUDE

Think of something you are *not* grateful for (maybe it's your neighbor's unkempt lawn or not feeling as healthy as you'd like to be). Write it down here.

_____

Now, think of some part of this thing that you *are* grateful for (maybe you're reminded of how much you love to garden or the good things your body can do). Write it down here:

_____

_____

Being grateful all the time isn't easy. But it's when you feel least thankful that you are most in need of what gratitude can give you: perspective.

~OPRAH WINFREY

NOTICE *the givers*

By recognizing those who serve you in your daily life, you'll find even more opportunities for gratitude and connection with others. Say thank you to someone who doesn't get thanked often—let them know they are seen and appreciated. Here are some examples:

BUS DRIVER · MAIL CARRIER · STOCKER AT THE SUPERMARKET
CUSTOMER SERVICE REPRESENTATIVE · GARBAGE TRUCK DRIVER

Who did you thank?

_____

How did they respond to your gratitude?

_____

_____

I feel
grateful
for...

content with what you have; rejoice in the way things are. When
you realize there is nothing lacking, the whole world belongs to you.

LAO TZU

forgive yourself

When we free our thoughts of criticism and blame, we can be open to forgiveness and gratitude. We can find room for delight. Think of something you feel guilty or ashamed about—something you said or did, or did not do. Remember that the things we tell ourselves affect how we see the world. Tell yourself that it is in the past, and that today is a new start. Give yourself permission to say goodbye and begin the process of forgiving yourself.

What in your life brings you guilt or shame? What have you learned about yourself because of it? How can you give thanks for its presence in your life?

Happiness
is a how;
not a what.

~HERMANN HESSE

discover gratefulness in everything

In times of sorrow, like the news of a serious illness, the loss of a loved one or a job, or the end of a relationship, we are struck with profound grief and pain. Yet it is through this pain that we emerge stronger, wiser, and lighter than before. Cancer survivors often report feeling unprecedented joy and gratitude for life and their loved ones. Life is certainly filled with joy and pain, but it is through giving thanks that we honor both.

I feel grateful for...

There are always flowers for those who want to see them.
HENRI MATISSE

release the tangles of stress

Buddhists believe that the suffering we experience in life can become internal knots. When we visualize untying these knots, we reduce stress and clear our mind to see the positive things in life. What knot do you need to untie? Starting in the middle of the opposite page, slowly draw a spiral, moving outward, while envisioning untying the stress in your life.

I feel grateful for...

...anks are the highest form of thought; and that gratitude ...appiness doubled by wonder. G. K. CHESTERTON

SPOT THE
gifts of life

Having gratitude implies you have been given gifts—
and your life is full of them. They could be big or small.
Maybe it's happy news from a friend, meeting a deadline,
or someone holding the door for you. What gifts were
you given today?

_____

_____

_____

practicing gratitude

Place simple reminders around you to give thanks. A sign on the fridge or your alarm clock that reads "I am grateful" can trigger you to redirect your day towards gratitude. Today, create a sign with a phrase that has special meaning for you, such as "Choose Happy" or "Seek Gratitude," and place it somewhere that you'll see it often, such as your mirror, car dashboard, or desk.

connect meaningfully

Plan a gratitude visit with someone—a family member, a friend, a teacher. Let them know you'd like to meet with them. Don't give the reason why just yet. Before the date, write down why you are grateful for them. When you arrive, bring your letter for them to keep, and read it out loud. You may be nervous—you both may be. Your nerves show your genuine care and thoughtfulness. People who have made gratitude visits, both the giver and receiver, say the positive feelings from them have lasted for weeks, even months after.

I feel grateful for...

y through our connectedness to others can we really know and
nance the self. And only through working on the self can we begin
enhance our connectedness to others. HARRIET LERNER

Someone's sitting in the shade today because someone planted a tree long ago.

~WARREN BUFFETT

celebrate togetherness

The concept of *ubuntu*, which originates from southern Africa, roughly means "I am what I am because of who we all are." We are all connected, and it's through our connectedness that we find ourselves, our common human spirit. When one suffers, we all feel pain. When we rejoice, we all celebrate—together. When we start to acknowledge the ways our lives are intertwined with the lives of those around us, our compassion and kindness grows.

offer hope FOR OTHERS

Connecting with and finding compassion for those around you allows love to grow and can even reduce stress in your own life. Think of someone who needs your compassion. What is something good you are hoping for them? Now, tell that person. Even a quick text, call, or email will do.

How did the person react?

_____

_____

How did you feel afterwards?

_____

_____

I feel grateful for...

ok back in forgiveness, forward in hope, down in compassion, and
with gratitude. ZIG ZIGLAR

CLEAR YOUR
body and mind

Practicing meditation or mindful relaxation allows your body and mind to appreciate your life more richly. Sit quietly for a few minutes and silently repeat a mantra that speaks to you. Here are some meditation mantras to try:

- I AM THANKFUL FOR THIS DAY AND ALL THE GIFTS GIVEN TO ME.
- I BREATHE IN JOY. I BREATHE OUT JOY.
- I AM GRATEFUL FOR FEARFUL MOMENTS, FOR THEY SHOW ME HOW MUCH COURAGE I HAVE.

Now try writing your own:

I feel grateful for...

e moment one gives close attention to anything, even a blade of
ass, it becomes a mysterious, awesome, indescribably magnificent
rld in itself. HENRY MILLER

define your place of joy

Certain places in your life can have a powerful way of giving you comfort. Many spiritual and therapeutic practices use visualization of places to increase well-being. By focusing your mind and body this way, you increase your overall focus in life and reduce stress. Try visualizing a place that brings you joy or peace. By envisioning your favorite place, your brain gets some of the same benefits as actually being there.

Describe a favorite place to be. It could be some-where you've been once, a place you often go, a place you wish to visit someday, or even an imagined place. What is it? How do you feel there? What are some of the objects around you? What's the weather like? Does anyone go there with you?

pause in wonder

When you look up at the stars, or look out from the top
of a mountain or skyscraper, it's easy to feel small and
insignificant. How fleeting our lives can be. How delicate
we are. It is in this feeling of smallness that we can see
how incredible it is to be alive. Right now. How lucky we
are to be here.

walk WITH INTENTION

Whenever you take a walk, keep an eye out for beautiful things, big and small, that you are grateful for. Maybe it's the sun shining on your shoulders, a smiling neighbor, the city noises, a flower growing in a sidewalk crack. List some of the things you notice below.

_____

_____

_____

_____

I feel grateful for...

the elements for your happiness are already here. There is no need

run, strive, search, or struggle. Just be. THÍCH NHẤT HẠNH

Find the good.
It's all around you.
Find it, showcase it
and you'll start
believing in it.

~JESSE OWENS

RECOGNIZE
your own gifts

IF YOU WERE AN ANIMAL, YOU'D BE MOST LIKE A...

- ☐ Cheetah, who is goal oriented, a quick learner, and empathetic.

- ☐ Dolphin, who is playful, harmonious, and strong.

- ☐ Honeybee, who is hardworking, a great communicator, and nurturing.

volunteer TO HELP

Gratitude protects us from focusing too much on ourselves, which can lead to depression and isolation. Turn your attention outward. By giving of yourself, you receive kindness and gratitude in return. Today, find an opportunity to volunteer to help others—maybe a small project at work, gardening for a neighbor, or buying coffee for a stranger.

What did you do to help others? How did it make you feel to give back? What did you notice about the person after you helped them?

I feel grateful for...

Gratitude is a vaccine, an antitoxin, and an antiseptic.
JOHN HENRY JOWETT

start a chain reaction

Gratitude can be an overwhelming feeling—in a good way. When we feel grateful for something, we can experience a powerful urge to connect with others and share the goodwill that we feel. This response turns into a chain of kindness, lifting our own well-being and deepening our relationships with others.

I feel grateful for...

moments of happiness we enjoy take us by surprise. It is
that we seize them, but that they seize us. ASHLEY MONTAGU

see beauty in others

When you receive a compliment from someone, you realize how just a few words can change the rest of your day. Give someone a compliment today—recognize their bright smile, sense of humor, or a wise thing they said. Their gratitude will reflect back to you and give you a sense of connection, which has been shown to boost your mood and even your self-perception.

WHO DID YOU COMPLIMENT TODAY?

recognize your riches

Imagine the burdens you *don't* have in your life that make you grateful for what you *do* have. Perhaps you don't have to worry about finding a comfortable place to sleep tonight. Or you don't have chronic pain that distracts you from enjoying life. You don't have to worry about tsunamis, famines, or fresh drinking water. Thinking of things you don't have to worry about allows you to see how fortunate you really are.

What are some things that you *don't* have that you are grateful for? Do you know anyone who has these burdens? What are some ways that you might be able to help?

I feel grateful for...

ppiness cannot be traveled to, owned, earned, worn or consumed. ppiness is the spiritual experience of living every minute with love, ace, and gratitude. DENIS WAITLEY

Trade your
expectations for
appreciation and
your whole world
changes instantly!

~TONY ROBBINS

remember others' intentions

Sometimes our plans flop. We get disappointed. Maybe a loved one caused you anger or sadness, or a coworker criticized your project. It's hard to find gratefulness in these moments. But everything has a gift inside of it, even if it's not what we expected. We can turn disappointments around by seeing what was intended. Perhaps your friend was trying to help you grow, or your coworker was trying to make your work the best it could be. We may not be able to change what happened. But we can challenge ourselves to imagine the goodness that people intend to bring us, even if it doesn't immediately feel that way.

REJOICE *with others*

Gratitude can help you to see that you wouldn't be where you are without those around you. Write down three things in your life that you are proud of—these could be accomplishments, possessions, or experiences. WHO HELPED YOU ACHIEVE THESE?

I feel grateful for...

on a deeper level you are already complete, and when you
realize that, there is a playful, joyous energy behind what you do.

ECKHART TOLLE

share YOUR GRATITUDE

START A GRATITUDE JAR: Place a jar in a prominent spot, and put money in it whenever you feel grateful for something. It could be as little as pennies. You'll start to notice just how quickly it fills up and becomes a reminder of all the things you are grateful for. Once the jar is full, donate the amount to a favorite charity.

I feel grateful for...

me, every hour is grace. And I feel gratitude in my heart each time I can meet someone and look at his or her smile. ELIE WIESEL

honor a true friend

The word *namaste* has many meanings, one of them being "the light in me sees the light in you." It is a greeting to friends, acknowledging the goodness we each hold in our hearts. A true friend is one that sees you as you are, clearly, without negative judgment, and offers you loving kindness.

Who in your life is a true friend? Who sees you for who you are? Use the space below to give thanks for their gift of recognition and acceptance. Then, if you'd like, share your gratitude with them in person.

take steps with grace

The practice of using movement to heal has been around a long time and is used all around the world. Walking meditations have shown to reduce stress and boost your overall well-being. The key is to keep it slow and simple, always directing your attention back to your feet moving along the ground, your breath moving in and out at its own unique pace, and keeping your thoughts clear. Just a few minutes of mindful walking can allow you to find peace and appreciation for the present moment.

LOOK *forward*

From upcoming events to unknown adventures, you have much to look forward to. The future is full of gifts. Visualizing your positive future has been shown to give you a greater chance of it actually becoming real. NAME SOME GOOD THINGS YOU SEE IN YOUR FUTURE.

_____

_____

_____

_____

_____

I feel grateful for...

tend to forget that happiness doesn't come as a result of getting something we don't have, but rather of recognizing and appreciating what we do have. FRIEDRICH KOENIG

Happy are those who evolve from within.

~AMIT ABRAHAM

remember YOUR BODY'S GIFTS

Your body is working hard to move you through your day. Each motion it takes is a gift to you. Take a look at one part of your body you don't normally pay attention to, such as your hands or your nose. Name five things that it did today. Give thanks for what it has given you.

_____

_____

_____

_____

_____

fulfill YOUR DREAMS

Aspiring to reach long-term goals is a common attribute in happy people. Perhaps it's to start your own business. To pay off debt. To learn to surf or to watch your child graduate from college. It's easy to think of them as distant goals, yet there are ways to link your future with today. Even small, steady steps now will lead to greater satisfaction and gratitude later. START THINKING ABOUT HOW YOU CAN HELP YOUR GOALS EMERGE.

What is one of your long-term goals? What are some small things you can do today to begin achieving it? Who can help you reach your goal?

_____

_____

_____

_____

_____

_____

_____

_____

_____

_____

_____

_____

_____

_____

_____

_____

I feel
grateful
for...

...ppiness is not out there for us to find. The reason that it's ... out there is that it's *inside* us. SONJA LYUBOMIRSKY

make the most of your time

Imagine you are visiting Paris for the first time. You have one week to see and do everything you'd like to do. See the Eiffel Tower. Eat croissants. Drink espresso. Walk through Notre Dame. Where do you begin? We are all visitors here, and even in our everyday lives we have lots to do. Create your itinerary for each day, and let it guide your actions and thoughts. Be thankful for this trip of a lifetime and all that it has to offer.

I feel grateful for...

s being human is a guest house. Every morning a new arrival. RUMI

give yourself credit

Turn your gratitude inward. Write something that you are grateful for, and then connect it with something within you that brought you to it. For example: "I love my friends. I am grateful that I have the ability to find good people to surround me." Or: "I'm excited about my new home. I'm grateful for my ability to recognize a good place for me to live." WHAT ARE SOME WAYS THAT YOU BRING GOODNESS INTO YOUR LIFE?

see the builders of your life

Name ten people who helped create your home and everything in it. These can be known friends and family or unknown people such as those who cut the wood for the lumber, the movers who packed your boxes, or the farmers who grew your vegetables. Give thanks for those who worked together to build your home.

trace how you got here

You are here now. What you have left behind is a path that only you have taken. It's a path with ups and downs, unexpected turns, and possibly some heartbreak or tragedy. And yet here you are. Which means you've endured and are wiser and stronger than before. More appreciative. You couldn't have done it without your unique path. Give thanks to the road you have taken and all that it encompasses.

What is a painful memory in your life? This could be something from the past or something you are experiencing now. Can you try to see it in another light? What gifts has it brought you? How has your perspective changed because of it?

I feel grateful for...

sn't what you have or who you are or where you are or what ⅃u are doing that makes you happy or unhappy. It is what you ⁱk about. DALE CARNEGIE

Gratitude is
an opener
of locked-up
blessings.

~MARIANNE WILLIAMSON

see where happiness lies

You have been in pursuit of happiness, and yet it has been in you all along. It has been waiting for you to recognize it, to let it shine within you. Happiness is not something to find, but rather, to recognize in the everyday. In the quiet moments of rest and even in the moments of disappointment and sorrow. It is your reality reframed. HAPPINESS IS YOU.

ENJOY
THE *little things*

Gratitude can be found even in the smallest things. A thumbtack holding a picture of your family. A cup full of clean water for you to drink. A key that opens the door to your home. Find three small things you can see around you right now, and imagine how they add goodness to your life. Write them down here.

_____

_____

_____

I feel grateful for...

hat we call little things are merely the causes of great things...

NRI-FRÉDÉRIC AMIEL

With special thanks to the entire Compendium family.

FOR LEE, THANK YOU FOR THAT HIKE IN OCTOBER TO OUR FAVORITE TREE.
—MIRIAM

CREDITS:
Written by: Miriam Hathaway
Designed by: Sarah Forster
Edited by: Amelia Riedler & M.H. Clark

Photography by: FRONT AND BACK COVER: ROB BYE / UNSPLASH; PAGE 2: © [ARTVERAU] / DOLLAR PHOTO CLUB; PAGE 9: © [VERA KUTTELVASEROVA] / DOLLAR PHOTO CLUB; PAGE 10: FFWDI / PHOTOCASE.COM; PAGE 16: TYSSUL PATEL / UNSPLASH; PAGE 28: DEMI KWANT / UNSPLASH; PAGE 33: TRENT HANCOCK / UNSPLASH; PAGE 38: MISTERQM / PHOTOCASE.COM; PAGE 42: © [SCISETTI ALFIO] / DOLLAR PHOTO CLUB; PAGE 46: PSYCHOLYCHEE / PHOTOCASE.COM; PAGE 55: STEFFIVD / PHOTOCASE.COM; PAGES 56–57: © [ES75] / DOLLAR PHOTO CLUB; PAGE 62: ROWAN HEUVEL / UNSPLASH; PAGE 72: CARÖLCHEN / PHOTOCASE.COM; PAGE 76: .FAUN. / PHOTOCASE.COM; PAGE 83: TOMAS BANKAUSKAS / UNSPLASH; PAGES 90–91: © [DMITRY] / DOLLAR PHOTO CLUB; PAGE 98: ANANDA ESCUDERO GOMES / UNSPLASH; PAGE 104: PENCAKE / PHOTOCASE.COM; PAGE 108: ANNIE SPRATT / UNSPLASH; PAGE 119: JOTO / PHOTOCASE.COM; PAGE 124: DENKERHAUS / PHOTOCASE.COM; PAGES 128–129: © [TETIANA ZBRODKO] / DOLLAR PHOTO CLUB; PAGE 140: SARAH FORSTER; PAGE 147: TAVIN DOTSON / UNSPLASH; PAGE 150: IDELLA MAELAND / UNSPLASH; PAGE 162: FANIEMAGE / PHOTOCASE.COM; PAGE 169: VICTOR FILIPPOV / UNSPLASH.

ISBN: 978-1-943200-01-6

5th printing. Printed in China with soy inks.